The Butler's Story

The extraordinary life and crimes of Archibald Thomson Hall

Murder World Scotland

Book 4

Murder World: Real crimes, real killers.

Table of Contents

Introduction 4
Prologue 7
Chapter 1: Establishing shots 9
Chapter 2: Ambition 20
Chapter 3: First Intermission 28
Chapter 4: The Servant 35
Chapter 5: Second Intermission 41
Chapter 6: Man of affairs 47
Chapter 7: A Shot in the Dark 55
Chapter 8: Murder most foul 65
Chapter 9: A matter of life and death 72
Chapter 10: Beyond a reasonable doubt 80
Chapter 11: Fade Out 86
Conclusion 94
Bibliography 99
About the Author 102
Other Murder World Scotland books 103

Copyright © 2018 by Steve MacGregor - All rights reserved.

No part of this book or any portion thereof may be reproduced or transmitted in any form or by any means, electronic or mechanical, including photocopying, recording, or by any information storage and retrieval system without the written permission of the author or publisher, except where permitted by applicable law.

Introduction

'*The butler did it*' is probably one of the best known clichés of British detective fiction. The thing is, it isn't true – the butler was almost never the murderer in any book published during the Golden Age of British detective fiction (1920s/1930s) other than in a single novel, *The Door*, a novel by then best-selling author Mary Roberts Rinehart in 1930. US author and crime fiction authority S. S. Van Dine even warned against making the butler the culprit in his 1928 essay *Twenty Rules for Writing Detective Stories*. Rule eleven reads:

> "Servants--such as butlers, footmen, valets, game-keepers, cooks, and the like--must not be chosen by the author as the culprit. It is a too easy solution. It is unsatisfactory, and makes the reader feel that his time has been wasted. The culprit must be a decidedly worth-while person--one that wouldn't ordinarily come under suspicion; for if the crime was the sordid work of a menial, the author would have had no business to embalm it in book-form."

However, in real-life, some crimes actually were the 'sordid work of a menial'. Scotsman Archibald Thomson Hall, who also liked to be known as Roy Hall and Roy Fontaine, was a complicated person. A bisexual con-man, occasional butler and multiple murderer, he was one of the very few prisoners in a British jail to be sentenced to a whole life tariff – i.e. a sentence which meant that he would remain in prison until he died. He spent his time in prison telling stories about himself to anyone who would listen and writing his autobiography which was published in the UK and elsewhere.

In his autobiography, Hall modestly explained that he was a man of irresistible sexual charisma (to both sexes), a cultured person who appreciated the finer things in life, an accomplished jewel thief, a con-man, prison escapee and an all-round lovable rogue. Who had, unfortunately, been forced by circumstances beyond his control, to kill five people. Reading his own version of the story, it's easy to imagine Roy Fontaine as a sort of Ted Bundy character played by Cary Grant in a film version of his life directed by Alfred Hitchcock, but the truth is a little different.

Hall was a bungling, incompetent and vicious criminal who became entranced with a Hollywood version of what the good life ought to look like. He spent his whole life trying to attain this vision but failed spectacularly – he had already been sentenced to more that forty years in prison before he was finally convicted of three murders. He lived a fantasy life based on the assumption of a number of different roles, just like the film stars he admired so much - even the names he assumed were taken from film stars of the day.

He was found to have severe mental health issues on a number of occasions and was a brutal and ruthless murderer and a tireless self-publicist who reveled in the notoriety that his convictions and long sentences brought him. The murders he committed were not forced on him by circumstances as he claimed, they were the result of a combination of his own short-sighted stupidity, a ruthless indifference to the suffering of his victims and a desire to find instant solutions to his problems.

This butler not only did it more than once, he appeared to enjoy it too.

> Note: The quotations which introduce each chapter come from The *Psychodynamic Diagnostic Manual,* a psychology textbook used in the US and these are descriptions of the characteristics of people who suffer from Psychopathic Personality Disorder.

Prologue

For almost fifty-three years Archibald Thompson Hall used nothing more violent than deceit, charm and an ability to turn himself into a number of different characters to dupe the unwary into parting with their money. He posed as everything from an Arab Sheik to a British Lord and he was convincing enough in these roles to be able to pull off some audacious confidence tricks. He was a consummate actor who was able to play the disparate characters required for his deceptions with ease and conviction. Even in his personal life, he briefly played the roles of a happily married man, a dutiful son, a master criminal and a man in love in addition to his famous portrayal of a cultured and well-spoken servant. If life had treated him differently, it's very easy to imagine Hall having a successful career on the stage or even in the movies that he adored.

Instead, he dedicated himself to a life of instant gratification and crime. When no obvious deception was available, he resorted to simple robbery and burglary when required. He wasn't a particularly successful criminal, as attested to by the fact that he spent more than half of his adult life in prison, but the one thing he didn't do, ever, was to use violence in the commission of his crimes.

Then, in late 1977, he murdered his ex-lover in an argument over a planned robbery. Later that year and within a period of little more than two months he brutally killed four more people and, if he hadn't been caught, he would almost certainly have killed more. When he began to kill, he wasn't just ruthlessly efficient, he also seems to have been entirely untroubled by his conscience. He not only felt no pity for his victims as he killed them, he felt no remorse or regret afterwards.

What happened? Just what was it that caused this affable con-man to turn into a serial killer? To try to understand the answer, it's necessary to look at the life of Archibald Hall, not just at his career as a murderer. So, let's raise the curtain by travelling back to the streets of Govan in Glasgow in the 1930s…

Chapter 1: Establishing shots

> 'Deceitfulness, as indicated by repeatedly lying, use of aliases, or conning others for personal profit or pleasure.'

The notion that he was born into *'grinding poverty'* in Glasgow has become part of the Archibald Thompson Hall legend, mainly due to his own recounting of his life story. However, like many other parts of his autobiography, this doesn't stand up to any rational analysis.

Hall was the son of Archibald Snr, who worked in the central Post Office in George Square in Glasgow, and Marion who worked as a waitress at the prestigious Malmaison restaurant in the Central Hotel. He was born in 1924 and before he started school, the family moved to Maclean Street in Govan on the south side of Glasgow, not far from the River Clyde and Ibrox football stadium.

Govan was a solidly working class area, but it was very different to other areas of Glasgow such as Gorbals where there really was constant violent crime and extreme poverty. Many people in Govan worked in the nearby shipyards. This was tough work, but it paid comparatively well and skilled men brought home a wage packet that was sufficient to feed, clothe and house their families comfortably. In the 1920s the shipyards of Clydeside were booming, replacing merchant and naval vessels destroyed during the First World War and even during the recessions of the 20s and 30s, unemployment wasn't such a major issue in Govan as it was in other parts of Scotland.

A Clydeside shipyard. This is the A & J Inglis yard and the ship closest to the camera is the Clyde paddle steamer Jeanie Deans.

Photo: A. & J. Inglis

However, the Hall family were a step up even from their neighbors and in comparison to most families in Maclean Street they must have appeared respectably middle class. Hall also claimed in his autobiography that his family owned their house in Govan, but this seems to be no more than a piece of wishful thinking given that the family had no independent means and it was almost impossible for a working-class family to obtain a mortgage in the 1930s.

Hall's father was a staunch Presbyterian, though by all accounts an easy-going, not especially ambitious and rather humorless man who was perfectly content with his life. Hall's mother was the direct opposite in that she never felt comfortable living amongst the grubby shipyard workers of Govan. She had aspirations towards the arts, though she never seemed to have quite decided how to express this (she claimed that she would have liked to have been an actress, though she had never actually tried it). She wasn't particularly popular with other people in the local area, which was probably unsurprising in that she made it clear that she felt that she and her family were rather superior to their neighbors. She spent time listening to the radio and trained herself to lose her Glaswegian accent by copying the pronunciation of the BBC announcers. She also sprinkled her conversation with French words and phrases because, she claimed, the French were innately more sophisticated and more cultured than the British.

Marion made sure that her young son copied her accent and she stressed to him that he must never lower himself to become one of the hordes of boiler-suited, rough-spoken men who daily made their way through the streets of Govan to the shipyards. He was special, she told him, he must aspire to the finer things in life and shrug off his humble beginnings. He was born to ride in luxury on the great ocean liners, not to build them.

She always called her son "*Archibald*", never "*Archie*", and she insisted that others did the same. She became especially angry when people referred to him as the Glaswegian diminutive "*Erchie*", and incandescently angry when father and son were called "*Big Erchie*" and "*Wee Erchie*" by people on Maclean Street.

It was clear that Marion Hall felt trapped in Govan and by what she felt to be her ordinary life and marriage. Like many other mothers before and since, she tried to find fulfillment by encouraging her child to escape from his life among the common people. However, instead of inspiring him to find a way out, she simply persuaded her son feel that he was, in some indefinable way, entitled to the finer things of life. This helped to foster a constant, nagging sense of dissatisfaction in the boy, a feeling of not really belonging that would follow Hall throughout his life.

Unfortunately, having persuaded her son that he was destined for better things, Marion did nothing to equip him to achieve this. Archibald had no special talents or skills that would boost him to a better life and the Hall family was unable to afford the sort of private education that might have helped. Young Archibald was left unhappy with his life and unable to see any conventional route that would take him to a new role where he would spend time on those great ocean liners.

Perhaps unsurprisingly, Archibald grew up a loner with few close friends at school. The other children mocked him because he used his *"posh"* voice while talking to teachers but spoke the same as the rest of them in the playground. Hall had indeed learned that, if he spoke in his BBC accent to his teachers, they responded well even if he didn't put much effort into his studies. Charm, the young Archibald Hall was learning, could be used as an alternative to hard work if it was focused and used in the right places. This was one lesson from his schooldays that he was to remember throughout his life.

Hall's father mocked him for his lack of friends and tried to get him to join the Boy's Brigade or the Boy Scouts, but young Archibald wasn't keen. Neither was his mother who felt that it was best to keep her son as far as possible from the corrupting influence of local children.

Hall began to read widely, though not the material that was required by his teachers or the bible study favored by his father. He became fascinated by the writings of Aleister Crowley, the self-styled *"most evil man in the world."* Crowley founded a Satanic religion known as Thelema which included something known as '*sex magic*' which required the participation of attractive young women to ensure that spells worked properly. This proved to be a very popular concept with male occultists in the 1920s and 1930s, though sadly, it did not seem to hold the same appeal for attractive young ladies. To enable his followers to perform the magic rituals Crowley was forced to introduce the slightly disappointing idea of '*masturbatory magic*'. Despite this, Crowley's writings continued to appeal to the dispossessed, the discontented and to complete dingbats everywhere.

One of the things that attracted young Archibald to Crowley's writing was the concept that certain people were so powerful, talented and extraordinary that the normal rules and laws of society did not apply to them ('*Do what thou will*' became the only rule for Crowley's followers). This complete amorality appealed greatly to Hall and was something that he was to remember throughout his life.

There was one last thing that Hall claimed to have learned from his reading of Crowley's work, and that was the value of what some people described as the '*basilisk stare*', a ferociously frightening, unblinking glare that Crowley employed when charm failed to deliver what he wanted. This was said to be so terrifying that Crowley was able to use it to dominate anyone who tried to oppose him. Hall was physically unprepossessing and was generally unable to use physical coercion to achieve his aims. Instead, he spent time practicing an unblinking glare in the mirror and attempted to use this whenever he needed to subdue someone who wouldn't succumb to his glib charm.

Aleister Crowley demonstrates his *'basilisk stare'*

Photo: *The Equinox* Volume 1, Issue 10 (1913)

In addition to Crowley, Hall was also impressed with the Fascist leaders Benito Mussolini and Adolf Hitler. Both were rising to power in the 20s and 30s and, it seemed to Hall, had acquired absolute power through little more than the force of their personalities. This accorded closely with the teachings of Crowley and was a very attractive proposition for a young man who felt he was destined for better things but had no means of attaining them in any conventional way. Hall was also fond of pointing out that he and Adolf Hitler shared a set of initials: AH. Surprising though it may seem now, admiration for Hitler was fairly common in the Glasgow of the 1930s, mainly amongst those naïve enough to assume that National Socialism had anything at all to do with actual socialism.

By the late 1930s, the teenaged Hall was convinced that his mother was right and that he didn't belong in the tenements of Govan. He began to indulge in a rich fantasy life in which he escaped to more congenial surroundings and these often involved his going to America. This was partly fuelled by the plethora of American movies which were being shown in local cinemas. Hall, like almost every other child in the UK in the 1930s, was brought up on a steady diet of American gangster and western films. He loved going to the movies where, for a short time, he could immerse himself in a world which was more glamorous, more exciting and more dramatic than his own.

He watched films avidly in local cinemas including the luxurious La Scala on Sauchiehall Street where patrons could drink, smoke and eat a three-course meal while watching a movie. He loved to see the material opulence in which all celluloid Americans seemed to live and he envied them their fine clothes, big cars, good food and drink. That was what he wanted! It wasn't long before he decided that he needed to do something about a particular issue that he felt was holding him back in his quest for a better life.

Hall hated his Christian name. He was not, he told himself, really an Archibald. Someone called Archibald belonged in Govan. He did not. Therefore, he was clearly not an Archibald. He decided that needed a new name which would make this clear to everyone. He had actually already considered several possible alternatives. He was particularly fond of the Arabian Nights stories which his mother had told him as a young child. His favorite character was Sinbad, and as a young teenager he had seriously considered telling people that was his name (this also related to his reading of Crowley – a name comprising '*sin*' and '*bad*' sounded ideal to Hall). Fortunately, because calling himself Sinbad would likely have seen him tarred and feathered on the cobbled streets of Govan, he eventually decided on a less dramatic but equally satisfactory name change.

The inspiration came to him at the age of fourteen while watching a western film, *Under Western Skies,* at a local cinema. The star of the film was Roy Rogers, the singing cowboy, in his first leading role. Inspiration struck Hall - that was the answer! From now on, plain old Archibald Hall would become the more dashing and sophisticated sounding Roy Hall.

Roy Rogers with Mary Hart in a studio publicity shot.

Photo: Republic Pictures

When Archibald/Roy broke the news to his parents that evening, they were less than impressed, especially his father who clearly considered Archibald to be a perfectly adequate name. The teenager would not be deflected. Roy wasn't even Roy Rogers real name, he explained – he had been christened as the rather less heroic sounding Leonard Slye! And the only Archibald in Hollywood (Archie Leach) had only prospered when he changed his name to Cary Grant. The name Archibald was clearly an impediment to the kind of life that Hall intended to lead. If actors could change their names to something else, why couldn't he? His mind was made up: from now on, he was Roy and he would accept no argument.

His mother softened when he explained that Roy was French for '*King*' (Roi). That seemed to confirm that he was indeed special and it was therefore far more appropriate than the plebian "*Archibald*". His mother promptly agreed that she would now refer to him as Roy and tell all her friends and neighbors to do the same. His father, doubtless feeling more than a little slighted by this attack on his own Christian name, refused and continued to call his son "*Archie*" for the rest of his life, to the intense irritation of Roy and the bemusement of most other people.

Not for the last time, Roy Hall reinvented himself as a different character and used a combination of charm, bullying and tenacity to ensure that those around him went along with it. He became, in effect, a character actor, taking on new roles and new names when it suited him to do so. Soon it would be time for him to slip into the role of the loveable rogue, one that he felt suited his talents well and which might even enable him to escape from his humble beginnings without the inconvenient necessity to do anything as banal as beginning a career.

Chapter 2: Ambition

'Having a higher than normal physiological threshold for stimulation and therefore seeking it addictively.'

Roy was afflicted by an unfortunate combination of being extremely impatient and incorrigibly lazy – the idea of working at something for months or even years before it paid off was anathema to him. He wanted things that provided instant gratification with a minimum of effort. After all, if he was entitled to better things, why should he have to work for them? Sadly, the rest of the world didn't seem to recognize Roy's entitlement to a better life and he was left puzzling how to achieve his ambitions. Almost inevitably, this led him into a life of crime. However, the first time that he was caught breaking the law wasn't for personal gain, he claimed that it was to hurt his mother who he believed had betrayed him and his father!

At around the same time that Roy Hall assumed his new name and persona, his parents adopted a new daughter. Marion was apparently unable to have more children after giving birth to Roy, but in 1938 she and her husband adopted a six-year old girl, Violet. Both parents doted on the little girl and it might have been expected that Roy would have felt at least a little resentful at a popular new sibling, but that doesn't seem to have been the case.

Roy adored his little sister and she gave him the opportunity to indulge some awkward feelings that were beginning to emerge. Roy loved jewelry. Not the heavy rings that local ship workers sometimes wore, but the kind of things that he admired on the heroines in his favorite films. Diamond necklaces, jeweled ear-rings, tiaras. These became, in Roy's mind, inextricably linked with his notions of a better life and he began to fantasize about owning (and perhaps wearing) such things.

Having a little sister allowed him to indulge these fantasies by dressing her and her dolls in jewelry – not the real thing obviously, but sparkling toys that partly satisfied Roy's growing craving for bling. Roy also made dresses for his little sister's dolls – he was fascinated by the clothes that the female movie stars he admired wore and this was a way to indulge his interest without provoking a sudden and probably violent reaction from the locals if he tried wearing these things himself.

Then, in September 1939, everything changed. German forces entered Poland and on 3rd September the British Prime Minister Neville Chamberlain broadcast via radio to the nation what must be one of the least rousing calls to arms ever made in which he mentioned, almost in passing, that *"consequently, this country is at war with Germany"*.

For many people in Britain, the first few months of the war brought little change, but for the Hall family it was different. Archibald Hall was called up from his job at the Post Office to become a telegraph operator in the army and he and his family moved from Glasgow to an army camp at Catterick Garrison in North Yorkshire.

New recruits at Catterick Garrison in 1940 learn how to load the *'Boche Buster'*, an 18 inch railway gun.

Photo: Imperial War Museum

Sergeant Hall settled into his new job in the army without any major drama while Marion created her own drama by starting a torrid affair with an army Major. While his father seemed oblivious, young Roy was aware of what his mother was up to, and he wasn't happy about it. Later, he claimed he was angry because his mother was betraying his father.

However, given the fact that he generally viewed his father with contempt, it seems rather more likely that he was angry because he felt that his mother was betraying him.

The officer in question, Major Morris, was in the habit of entertaining Marion in the Officer's Quarters in the camp. Roy spotted his mother going there late one evening in the arms of the amorous Major. Much later, Roy would claim that he decided immediately that he needed to get rid of Major Morris. His plan, he said, was simple and pure Hollywood – he would break into the records office in the camp, steal secret papers and then plant them in Major Morris' quarters before informing the Military Police.

It was an audacious plan for a sixteen year old fantasist whose only knowledge of breaking and entering came from watching films. I suspect that it is also mainly a piece of fictional hindsight intended to make Roy look bold and clever. This story is one that he often told and it is repeated in several books and articles about him. However, in his autobiography Roy told a slightly different version of this story, where he had been undertaking petty theft from a number of officers in the camp for some time before he was caught by MPs who raided his family's quarters. In both versions, Roy claimed that he was caught with books by Crowley and Nazi memorabilia in his room, and that as a result the whole family were sent back to Glasgow in disgrace.

The truth is more difficult to discern. The Hall family certainly retuned to Glasgow after a relatively short time at Catterick. Archibald returned to his job at the Post Office and the family moved into rented rooms in a large house close to the University. However, it is very difficult to see how Roy being caught with stolen confidential documents and Nazi memorabilia would have resulted in his father being thrown out of the army. That just doesn't make sense - the official reason was that Roy's father was too old for military service, but this doesn't make sense either because this fact must surely have been known before Archibald Senior enlisted? What is true is that Marion gave birth to a son a little less than nine months after returning to Glasgow – Roy claimed that his new brother Donald was actually a half-brother who had Major Morris for a father though this was never admitted by his parents.

Roy was certainly responsible for some bungling attempt at theft while he was in Catterick and his age meant that he couldn't be prosecuted in an adult court. Instead, when the family arrived back in Glasgow, he was sent for psychological testing which noted that he was delusional, amoral, anti-social and prone to acting out his fantasies. It was suggested that Roy should be encouraged to undertake some activity for the public good in the hope that this would help to re-integrate him into society.

Roy thought that sounded like a fine idea and he claims that he approached the headquarters of Lady Pettigrew in Glasgow, the centre of a number of money raising schemes to help the war effort. Roy was given a Red Cross tin and sent out on to the streets of Glasgow to collect money for the war wounded. Making sure that he was always neatly dressed and polite, Roy proved to be very good indeed at collecting money. He even gave some of it to the Red Cross. He made a second collecting tin, for which he used the first as a model. He then used one of the tins to collect coins and the other to collect notes. The coins he handed in to the charity. The notes he kept for himself.

He generally used the tin for coins when he was collecting in poorer areas of the city and the tin for notes when he went collecting in affluent areas of the west end such as Westmuir. He hinted that he also used his collecting visits as an opportunity to case the homes of wealthy people with a view to burglarizing them later, though I'm not certain that the teenaged Roy ever actually committed any burglaries.

The episode of the Red Cross tins (and we must remember that we only have Roy's account of this) may have been true and, if it was, it is significant because it represents the first time that Roy did something illegal and immoral. And, according to him, it paid off handsomely and he was never caught.

Glasgow Cross, scene of some of Roy's collecting for the Red Cross during World War Two.

In 1941, a Polish airman, thirty year old Captain Jackobosky was billeted with the Hall family in their home. A shortage of space meant that Roy Hall and Jackobosky were forced to share a bed-settee in the living room. The Polish Captain was intelligent, cultured, charming and an experienced and enthusiastic homosexual. Roy had girlfriends before that, but his experiences with women had not progressed beyond kissing and cuddling. With Jackobosky he was introduced for the first time to homosexual sex and discovered that he enjoyed it immensely. For the rest of his life Roy would remain a bisexual.

When Jackobosky left, Roy applied to join the Royal Navy as soon as he was eighteen. He was attracted both to the idea of travel and to the notion of spending time on ships with lots of sex-starved sailors. Sadly for this particular fantasy, his earlier scrape with the authorities in Catterick Garrison had left a record which suggested that Roy wasn't ideally suited to the armed services and his application was rejected.

Roy continued to while away the time in Glasgow with his collection box scam and petty theft until, one evening he was drinking in the bar of the Central Hotel when he was approached by an older man. This proved to be Vic Oliver, a radio entertainer who had become well-known for starring in the hit show *Hi, Gang*. Oliver (who would go on to be the very first celebrity featured on *Desert Island Discs*) was also the son-in-law of Winston Churchill and another enthusiastic homosexual who rather liked the look of young Roy Hall. Oliver asked Roy whether he might enjoy an expenses paid trip to London? Roy said that he would enjoy that very much and, in 1943, he travelled south for the first time.

Chapter 3: First Intermission

> *'Failure to conform to social norms as indicated by repeatedly performing acts that are grounds for arrest.'*

Roy Hall spoke extensively about this period in wartime London, both in his autobiography and in a later book, *The Butler Did It* by Paul Pender, which was based on a series of interviews with Roy in Full Sutton prison near York. Roy's stories about his time in the capital are certainly entertaining, but as with most things that he says, it's difficult to know how much is actually true.

Roy Hall claimed that Vic Oliver introduced him to a high-society homosexual world where he met and had sex with a number of prominent people including Oliver, Lord Boothby (later to become famous for his association with the Kray twins), playwright Terrence Rattigan and Lord Mountbatten. Roy also spoke about being employed as a serving boy (while wearing only a thong) at lavish men-only parties hosted by (amongst many others) Ivor Novello. During this period he also claimed to have spent time at Somerset Maugham's home.

Whatever the truth of Roy's time in London, in 1945, just as the war was ending, he returned to Glasgow for reasons that have never been adequately explained. He moved back into his parent's house. Whilst there, for the first time, Roy Hall was convicted of a crime.

Govan after World War Two was still a thriving and major shipbuilding centre.

Photo: Imperial War Museum

Roy's mother had become concerned when she hadn't seen Mrs Robertson, an elderly woman living in the same block, for some time. Knocking at the door produced no response so Roy offered to clamber along a window ledge and get into the flat to check that she was all right. He did this and found the old woman lying dead on her bed. Roy quickly searched the flat and found two shoeboxes crammed with banknotes hidden in a wardrobe. Just as he was counting the cash, another neighbor, Mr McLaughlin, a tram driver, broke down the front door and entered the flat. Roy managed to persuade McLaughlin that the two of them should split the two thousand pounds (a considerable sum in 1945) and leave one hundred pounds in the shoebox.

This was what they did and Roy was praised for his honesty in handing over the one hundred pounds. However, to Roy's horror, McLaughlin proved to be a melancholy drunk who blurted out details of the theft to anyone who would listen. It wasn't long before the police arrived at the flat in Govan and took Roy into custody.

Roy and McLaughlin were tried and quickly found guilty of stealing the money from the flat. However because of Roy's previous assessment of his mental health in Catterick, it was decided that he should be assessed again before sentencing. Roy claims that he was able to fool the psychologists into sending him to Woodilee Home for the Mentally Disturbed rather than to prison. Roy felt that he had been able to put one over on the authorities, though it is equally possible that the psychologists rightly found him to be deluded and mentally unstable.

Although the regime at Woodilee was considerably easier than it would have been in prison, it wasn't to Roy's taste at all and it wasn't long before he escaped by the simple expedient of donning a discarded boiler suit and cap which had been used by a painter and walking out of the gate. After a month on the run, Roy returned to the mental hospital and handed himself in.

During his period outside, Roy had also decided that it was time to make another change to his life, and once again it concerned his name. Roy, obviously, was fine, but Hall, well, on reflection it just wasn't exotic enough to reflect the cultured tastes of this young man. After being entranced by a showing of Alfred Hitchcock's film version of *Rebecca* starring Joan Fontaine, Roy decided to re-model himself once again, this time as Roy Fontaine.

After his release from the mental hospital, Roy Fontaine looked for some new way of making a living. In 1949 he settled on opening a shop, *The Bric-a-brac Emporium* on Ibrox Road. The shop sold all kinds of small household items and antiques both over the counter and to dealers in the south. However, Roy had discovered that the most economic means of replenishing stock was burglary, either by selling on in the shop items he had stolen himself or fencing items stolen by others.

Roy or his associates would burgle houses in the affluent

suburbs of Glasgow and the stolen items would either be sold in the shop or, if they were too easily identified, shipped south to be sold to unscrupulous dealers in London. For almost one year Roy made a good living from the shop but then the police came calling. They noted that much of the shop's stock also featured on their list of stolen property and in 1950 Roy was sentenced to one year in prison. This time he was sent to Barlinnie, one of Scotland's toughest prisons, rather than to a mental hospital.

HM Prison Barlinnie

Photo: Chris Upson

Roy Fontaine, as he now called himself, didn't have an easy time in Barlinnie. He was becoming increasingly effeminate in his behaviour and appearance, his painted nails and his excessive use of aftershave didn't endear him to many of

Barlinnie's *'hard-man'* occupants. However, he did meet another prisoner who seemed to share his love of culture and the finer things in life - John Wooton was an Englishman who was serving time for attempting to steal antiques from a Scottish country house where he had been pretending to be a butler. Roy was entranced at this notion – a butler was not only able to share the elegant and sophisticated lifestyle of his employer, he was also in an excellent position to steal it from him.

Wooton and Roy Fontaine immediately struck up a friendship which was to last for many years. In some ways this seemed unlikely – Wooton was older than Roy, not a homosexual, not in the least bit effeminate and an ex-boxing champion. But the two shared a desire for a better life and an intention of achieving this through crime – Wooton was an experienced con-man and thief. He explained to Roy that he had been rumbled in his masquerade as a butler when his employer suspected that something in the manner and deportment of his new employee wasn't quite right.

Roy Fontaine decided immediately that he would apply his considerable energy and intelligence to turning himself into the perfect butler. John Wooton presented him with a copy of *Roberts' Guide for Butlers and Other Household Staff*. This 1827 publication is one of the first commercial publications written by an African American and provides guidance for those who hope to become butlers and waiters and covers such essential topics as how to arrange the work routines for other servants, how to remove stains from clothing and how to effectively polish household items and furniture.

This essential reference work was supplemented when Roy also found an elderly copy of *Burke's Peerage* in the prison library. This book, first published in 1826, provides details of the antecedents, genealogy and members of the landed gentry families of the UK. Essential reading for a prospective butler no doubt, but perhaps a slightly surprising book to find in the library of one of Scotland's toughest prisons.

Roy studied these works avidly and, with the support and encouragement of Wooton, began to create another new role for himself, this time as Roy Fontaine, the imperturbable and cultured gentleman's gentleman.

Chapter 4: The Servant

> *'Consistent irresponsibility, as indicated by repeated failure to sustain consistent work behaviour or honour financial obligations.'*

Roy Fontaine and John Wooton were both released from prison in 1951. Roy moved back in with his parents while he prepared for his new role as a butler. He also introduced Wooton to his parents, and it was immediately obvious that Marion was attracted to the cultured Englishman. However, Roy's father Archibald Hall had become unwell and was being looked after by Marion, so there was little scope for the two to spend much time together.

Roy quickly realized that his lack of references was likely to be a problem if he was to apply for a job as a butler, but this was easily overcome. Roy stole embossed, high quality stationery from some of the best hotels in Glasgow and used this to write his own letters of reference in which described himself in glowing terms as reliable, honest and a very experienced butler. He assumed (correctly for the most part as it turned out) that the kind of people he would be dealing with wouldn't bother to actually follow up these references to check that they were true.

Roy's first job as a butler took him to a castle in the far north of Scotland, but this proved something of a disappointment. The Lord and master of the castle took a broad view of the duties of a butler and Roy found himself being required to undertake heavy and menial work which was not at all to his taste. He remained there only long enough to familiarize himself with the security arrangements (in an odd coincidence which was to affect many of Roy's ex-employers, the castle was burgled less than three weeks after he left) before he took up another position, this time with the wealthy Lord and Lady Warren-Connel in their house near the village of Balfron in Stirlingshire.

Photo: David Taylor

This was much more to Roy's taste. There was a large staff at the house, over who Roy had control and part of his duties involved cleaning Lady Warren-Connel's jewelry. This meant that Roy was not only able to handle exotic and expensive jewelry, which he rather enjoyed, it also gave him the opportunity to remove some of the smaller diamonds and replace them with cut-glass replicas prepared by an associate in Glasgow. He reasoned that, while people might notice the substitution of a large diamond in a necklace, they were much less likely to notice that some of the smaller gems in an arrangement had been swapped. He was right and he managed to appropriate a number of small stones while working for the Warren-Connels without anyone noticing.

Roy's future as a butler seemed assured until, as happened so often in his life, things were rudely interrupted when a policeman turned up. Fortunately, the Warren-Connels were not at home but the policeman explained to Roy that Glasgow Police had been in touch and had pointed out that the family's dapper new butler had a criminal record which involved both theft and fraud. It would therefore be his duty to inform Roy's employers as soon as they returned. Roy made sure that he was gone by the time that the Warren-Connels returned.

He once again teamed up with John Wooton and the two men robbed an antique shop in Edinburgh, with Roy posing as a rich Texan oilman and scooping valuable items into a briefcase while Wooton distracted the elderly female owner. The two men then moved to London and while there, Roy robbed a smart hotel with the assistance of a safe-cracker. This went well until Roy's colleague got drunk and started telling people about the successful job. Once again, Roy's life was interrupted by the heavy tread of police boots approaching his apartment.

Roy was convicted of burglary and sentenced to a lengthy stay in prison. He served his time first in Parkhurst on the Isle of Wight and then in Nottingham prison where he was appointed prison librarian. Roy spent his time in Nottingham studying etiquette, antiques, history, wines - he still dreamed of returning to work as a butler as soon as he could. He even completed an external course run by a local college which qualified him as a sommelier! He became such an expert on matters of etiquette that the Governor consulted him more than once on the correct form of address for high-ranking visitors.

During his incarceration in Nottingham Roy received news that his father had died. He reacted with almost complete disinterest. The intervening years had not brought him any closer to his moral and religious father who felt that his son had disgraced the family – in contrast, his mother Marion still seemed to believe that her son's crimes were a manifestation of high spirits and were caused at least partly by her husband's refusal to encourage his son's creativity.

In 1963, Roy was released from prison and immediately set about creating a new set of Butler's references (noting that he had spent the last few years "*working abroad*"). He found it simple to find employment and moved from job-to-job for several months. He also met a woman called Phyllis Nye, a cook, and they began to apply for jobs together. The pair found work with Sir George and Lady Aylwen in an opulent apartment in Mayfair in London. However, Roy was keen to move onwards and upwards and when he became aware that the butler to Sir Charles Clore had become unwell, Roy applied for the position. Sir Charles was one of the wealthiest men in Britain and Roy assumed that there would be plenty of potential loot in his new employer's house.

He wasn't disappointed – during the interview he noted that Sir Charles had Picasso's on the wall and a Faberge egg worth at least half a million pounds in a cabinet. He and Phyllis Nye (who knew nothing about his criminal plans) got the job, but Sir Charles soon became suspicious of his new butler. Roy made one or two minor errors in etiquette which made his employer suspicious. Sir Charles assigned a private detective to look into Roy's past and to check his references.

It didn't take long to find out that most of his references were fictitious and in the cases of those that weren't, such as the Aylwen's, it had been found that several valuable but portable items had gone missing at around the same time that Roy had moved on. Roy was dismissed and Sir Charles passed on the report from his private detective to the police. In January 1964 Roy found himself once more in court and this time, as a result of his now extensive criminal record, he was sentenced to ten years in a high security prison. Once again, Roy's ambition to become the perfect butler had been interrupted.

Chapter 5: Second Intermission

'Taking pleasure in duping others and subjecting them to manipulation.'

Roy was sent to serve his sentence in Blundeston, a high-security prison near the North Sea and the city of Lowestoft in East Anglia. Blundeston was a high-tech prison that was claimed to be *"escape-proof"* – it was one of the first prisons in the UK to use CCTV cameras to monitor prisoners at all times and no-one had ever escaped before. Roy Fontaine was about to change all that.

HMP Blundeston

Photo: Evelyn Simak

One of the things that Roy noticed was that the CCTV

system could be switched to relay signals from television stations and that the guards often did this to relieve boredom. Roy waited until a day on which there were several FA Cup tie football matches on television, reasoning that on that day, the guards would most likely be using the prison's security system to watch television. He was right and Roy and two other prisoners were able to escape from Blundeston and to evade capture by improvising a raft on which they sailed down the River Waveny.

The three men stole a car and drove north to Glasgow where Roy had friends willing to give them money and a place to stay. Roy celebrated his escape with a champagne supper at his old local, the bar at the Central Hotel. The escape was covered in National newspapers which featured photographs of Roy, so he assumed that his chances of being able to obtain work as a butler were limited, at least until the immediate hue and cry died away. Instead, he and his new colleagues attempted to burgle a large house close to Glasgow. They not only failed, Roy was almost caught, so he decided that it might be best to remove himself to another part of the country. He went to Cornwall where he met up with John Wooton and the two robbed a jewelry shop by having Roy pose as Lord Menzies-Jones. They narrowly escaped with the loot and decided that it might be sensible to split up for a time.

Roy moved to London where he met Margaret, a single mother with a young child. Reasoning that the police were looking for a single man and would never suspect someone who appeared to be the father of a young child, Roy moved in with Margaret. However, taking work as a manservant was still too risky and, after two close-shaves, Roy was nervous about attempting another robbery. How was he to provide money for the three of them to live on?

After a great deal of deliberation, Roy settled on a scheme which involved taking on yet another role, this time as Sheik Medinah. Using a stolen credit card, Roy bought several expensive suitcases (which he stuffed with bricks and newspaper), rented Arab robes from a costume shop and hired a Rolls-Royce and a chauffeur for the day. He then stained his face and hands with iodine and made a reservation at the Dorchester Hotel in Mayfair where he and his impressively heavy luggage checked in as Sheik Mutlak Medinah.

Photo: Oxyman

The Dorchester Hotel had an expensive jewelry shop in the lobby and it wasn't long before the Sheik strolled in to take a look at the merchandise. However, he was unimpressed. These were not jewels worthy of a Sultan, didn't they have anything more appropriate? The manager fawningly promised to bring more exclusive items to the Sheik's suite.

When he arrived, the Sheik explained that it was necessary for him to take a bath, because he had been in such close contact with non-Muslims. He indicated a steaming bathtub in the large bathroom. Would it be possible for him to examine the items while he relaxed in his bath? The manager readily agreed and waited expectantly outside. After some time, he grew concerned, and knocked diffidently at the bathroom door. There was no response. He summoned hotel staff who were able to open the bathroom door for him. Inside there were a pile of discarded Arab robes on the floor, a sink stained with iodine where Roy had washed off his tan and an open door into an adjoining bedroom.

Roy, who had been wearing a smart suit under the robes, had long-since exited the hotel with a briefcase in which he later claimed had more than one million pounds worth of jewels. It seems likely that this is another piece of hyperbole. Roy certainly got away with some jewels, but not to the value of one million pounds – contemporary reports suggest something of the order of £150,000 and this would have been worth less than a quarter of that when fenced. However much he actually got, he used the proceeds of this scam to rent a detached house near Tunbridge Wells where he and Margaret lived as man and wife. He also bought himself a Jaguar, joined the local golf and Conservative clubs and settled down to a life of ease.

Roy did have to interrupt his new life briefly to travel back to Glasgow – in 1967 his mother had decided to re-marry and her new husband was John Wooton. Roy was delighted with this news and happy to see both of them. However, he was less happy to meet his younger brother Donald, who had just been released from prison in Glasgow following a conviction for petty theft. When Roy explained that he was planning a two-week holiday in Weston-Super-Mare when he returned to England, Donald asked if he could come too? Roy refused.

A few days later, police burst into Roy's hotel room in Weston-Super-Mare and arrested him. They had received, they told him, an anonymous tip that an escaped prisoner was spending a holiday there. Roy believed that it was Donald who had informed on him because he had not allowed his brother to join him on holiday, and though he never found any proof of this, his dislike and distrust for his younger brother (or half-brother, as he insisted) increased.

Roy found himself back in court and once again, he was sentenced to a further ten years in a high-security prison. He was sent back to Parkhurst on the Isle of Wight. He managed to behave himself there and after a few years he was transferred to the more congenial surroundings of Hull prison. Roy spent his time at Parkhurst and Hull continuing to study for a life as a butler. He even managed to complete a distance learning City and Guilds course in catering. When he got out of prison, he vowed, he would go straight and make a living not just by working as a butler, but by becoming the best butler in the world.

Chapter 6: Man of affairs

'Being charming and even charismatic.'

While he was serving time in Hull prison, something unexpected happened to Roy Fontaine. He fell in love with a handsome young thug called David Barnard. Barnard was in his twenties and Roy was in his mid forties but that, claimed Roy, wasn't a problem at all. Barnard was serving time for armed robbery and shooting a policeman and both men knew that Roy was likely to be released first. This was, Roy would later claim, the only time in his life that he ever truly fell in love.

HMP Hull

Photo: Paul Glazzard

At the same time in Hull, Roy also met and became involved with David Wright, a petty thief serving time in Hull who was keen to understand more about how to recognize, steal and fence valuable items such as jewels and antiques. Roy was happy to act as a tutor to the young man in exchange for sex.

This lasted until Roy was transferred to Preston low-security prison. Then, in 1970, he was released to a half-way house as part of the parole process, a grubby hostel which he hated. He was given a job in the kitchens of a local mental hospital, a job in which he did well, partly due to his new knowledge gained through his city and guilds course. His determination to go straight lasted precisely until he was put in charge of the hospital stores. He began to steal the stores and sell them on to the owner of a local shop, a widow named Hazel Patterson.

Hazel was charmed by Roy and it wasn't long before the two were engaged (Roy presented her with an impressive engagement ring which, in a romantic gesture, he had stolen especially for her). In 1972 Roy moved into Hazel Patterson's flat above the shop in Preston. While he was there, he helped out in the shop. Or at least, he did for some of the time because the truth was that Roy's life was becoming very complicated indeed.

Roy had also met an elegant and charming woman, Ruth

Holmes, during a visit to London. The two became very close and, also in 1972, they were married. For more than one year, Roy spent the week at Hazel Patterson's house in Preston before coming to London each weekend *'on business'*. Neither Ruth not Hazel knew anything about the other. For most people, that would have been quite complex enough, but during the same period, Roy was maintaining an affair with Mary Coggle, a Irish woman who had left her nine children behind to come and work in the UK as a cleaner at the mental hospital. Mary, also known as Belfast Mary, had issues with alcohol and was completely taken–in by Roy's stories.

Roy Fontaine around 1972

Roy claimed that he also used Mary to smuggle letters and other items to David Barnard and David Wright in Hull prison. At the same time, presumably to fill in any remaining idle moments, Roy was also having occasional clandestine meetings for sex with one of the (male) chefs who also worked at the mental hospital.

Things got even more complicated when Roy's mother persuaded Roy to give his brother Donald a job in Hazel's shop. Donald was having problems in Glasgow, mainly due to his inability to stay away from petty crime and a growing interest in very young girls which looked likely to send him back to prison. Marion hoped that, under the steadying influence of his older brother, Donald might be persuaded to settle down.

This didn't quite work out as planned. Donald had barely arrived in Preston when he attracted the attention of local police after stealing a Salvation Army tuba (something that Roy disgustedly described as the most pointless crime he had ever heard of). Police arrived at Hazel's shop to interview Donald but one of them recognized Roy as a man who he had seen at a charity event in London with his wife. His tall, blonde wife. The policeman looked at short, dark Hazel Patterson who suddenly seemed very confused indeed.

Somehow, Roy managed to persuade Hazel that the whole thing was nothing more than a terrible mistake, a story that was made more plausible when Ruth Holmes agreed to divorce him the following year. He also managed to persuade Hazel that it would be best if she sold her shop and if he took a job as a butler and she came along as a cook. She agreed, and in 1973, Roy was able to get them both jobs at Grimshaw Hall, a stately home in Warwickshire.

This earned Roy the undying enmity of Hazel's family and particularly her son Colin who believed (probably rightly) that Roy was simply interested in his mother's money. Roy's latest attempt to be the perfect butler was once again interrupted by the tread of heavy, official boots on the driveway. However, just for a change, this time it wasn't the police who were looking for Roy, it was MI5.

Earlier in 1973, Roy had met a handsome young man at the American Bar in the Savoy Hotel during a brief visit to London. He had charmed his new companion into bed and later noted that his new friend had a very impressive looking briefcase with official monograms on it. He stole it and discovered that it contained not valuables as he hoped but confidential papers from the Prime Minister's Office. Never one to miss an opportunity, he telephoned the Home Office and attempted to sell the papers back to them. When that was unsuccessful, he took the papers to the Russian Consulate in London and attempted to sell them to the Soviet Union. This was also unsuccessful and Roy failed to notice that the building was under surveillance by officers of MI5.

Roy found himself back in court where he was sentenced to four years in prison for contravening the Official Secrets Act. Many people were surprised that a habitual criminal should receive such a short sentence for such a serious conviction. Roy later claimed that his relatively light sentence was part of a plea bargain when he had threatened to reveal at the trial details of his wartime assignations with Lords Mountbatten and Boothby and his knowledge of the attendance of members of Ted Heath's government at a gay club in London. Whether this is true or not, Roy did seem to get off fairly lightly for attempting to sell official secrets.

Roy celebrated his fiftieth Birthday in Prison but, in 1974 he received bad news – David Barnard, his lover from Hull prison and, according to Roy, the only person he had ever really loved, was killed in a road accident. Then, in 1975 he received a visit from John Wooton with even worse news – Marion, his mother, was dead.

Roy later claimed that he was devastated by this news. It is certainly notable that, up to this time, Roy Fontaine had not used violence as part of any of his crimes. He later claimed that his mother was aware of all his crimes, but that she didn't condemn him for them because he didn't physically hurt anyone and because she saw his masquerades as an outlet for his frustrated creativity (something which only she had seen in her son). Whatever the truth of this, after his mother's death, Roy seemed more willing to employ violence.

In 1977, Roy was released from prison and went back to live with Hazel Patterson. He stayed with her until she had completely denuded her meager savings, then he decided it was time to move on once again. He told Hazel that he was going to work on oil rigs in the North Sea. In reality, he was planning to once again become a butler.

He answered an advertisement for a butler at Kirtleton House, the home of Lady Margaret Hudson in the Scottish Borders and not far from the village of **Waterbeck in Dumfriesshire**. Lady Hudson was seventy four years old but clearly no fool when it came to employment – after reading his letters of reference, she insisted on talking to Roy's previous employer. This required some fancy footwork on the part of Fontaine given that his previous employer wasn't a real person. He persuaded Lady Hudson to wait until the following day before calling what he claimed was the telephone number of *"Major Wooton"* - it was actually the number of a public telephone box and Roy made sure that he was waiting outside when the call came the next evening. He managed to persuade Lady Hudson not just that he was a retired army officer, but that his butler Mr Fontaine was a decent chap and an excellent butler. Roy was immediately taken on as the butler at Kirtleton House.

Lady Hudson had a number of valuable pieces, both jewelry and works of art, and Roy's plan was to wait for a while and then to rob her of as much as possible. He might even have been successful if it had not been for a letter which heralded the transition to next role he was to play, that of a multiple murderer.

Chapter 7: A Shot in the Dark

> *'Showing a lack of remorse, as indicated by being indifferent to or rationalizing having hurt, mistreated, or stolen from another.'*

Soon after he was settled in to a comfortable routine at Kirtleton House, Roy Fontaine received a letter from David Wright, one of his lovers from Hull prison. Wright had also been released and was bored, taking odd jobs to keep some money coming in. In November, Roy invited him for a weekend at Kirtleton House (after asking Lady Hudson's permission, as a good butler would).

Roy was walking with Wright in the grounds of the house when the pair met Lady Hudson. She was charmed by the young man and impulsively offered him a part-time job as a gardener on the estate. He accepted. Roy was happy, because he now had his lover within easy access, but also worried – Wright was a habitual petty thief and Roy didn't want anything to spoil his long-term plan to rob the house.

It wasn't long before Roy's concerns proved to be justified. David Wright (who, like Roy was bisexual) began an affair with Jeannie, a woman from the local area. One evening, Lady Hudson had gone away for the weekend and Roy was in the local bar when he met Jeannie. He noticed that she was wearing a large and very expensive ring. When he asked her where it had come from, she explained that it was a present from Wright. Roy knew immediately that it had been stolen from Kirtleton House and persuaded her to reluctantly give it back to him. Roy went back to the house, returned the ring and then he and David Wright had an acrimonious argument.

It wasn't that he was morally or philosophically against stealing Lady Hudson's possessions, Roy explained, but he was building up to a large-scale robbery that would bring in a healthy profit, and he didn't want Wright to put this at risk with petty theft. Wright, who had been drinking heavily, disagreed violently and demanded half the proceeds of the big robbery or he would tell Lady Hudson all about Roy's real background. He then went to the pub and Roy went to bed, still angry.

Then, according to Roy, he was woken in the early hours of the morning by a loud explosion in his bedroom. He realized that Wright, very drunk, was in the room and was brandishing a rifle which he had just fired into the headboard of Roy's bed. Roy was able to calm him and take the rifle. Wright almost immediately fell into a drunken sleep, leaving Roy to use filler to hide the bullet hole in his headboard and the wall behind.

Or at least, this was what Roy Fontaine later said had happened. But by then, he was doing his best to make his subsequent actions look like self-defence after Wright had threatened to expose him and fired a shot at him. No-one will ever be certain these things are true, but what we do know is that, the following day, Roy and David Wright went walking on the estate to shoot rabbits to feed Lady Hudson's dogs. During the walk, they sat down to have a cigarette and Roy shot Wright in the head at close range with a rifle. To his surprise, his victim didn't die immediately. Instead, Wright stood up and seemed to be trying to speak. Then blood gushed from his mouth and he sank to the ground, groaning and moving feebly. Just to be certain, Roy shot him five more times.

Photo: Alastair Seagroatt

When he was satisfied that Wright was dead, he concealed the body in undergrowth close to a small burn which ran across the estate. His main emotion, he said later, was anger that Wright had forced him to do this. He even claimed that Wright had been planning to kill Lady Hudson and that his death had protected her.

There was certainly no absolute need for Roy to kill his lover. Even if the story about Wright attempting to shoot him the night before was true, there was nothing to stop Roy simply moving on, something he had done many times before. Perhaps he felt that he was getting too old to keep constantly moving? Perhaps he really believed that robbing Kirtleton House would bring him so much wealth that he couldn't afford to let the opportunity slip? Or perhaps the death of his mother really had removed the last moral constraints on his actions and killing Wright was the simplest and easiest response to the problem?

He returned to Wright's body that evening and buried it in the bed of the small burn. He then took one of Lady Hudson's dogs for a walk in the area, to check whether it would find the body. It did. He re-buried the body deeper in the stream bed and returned with the dogs. This time, they ignored the spot. He explained Wright's absence by telling Lady Hudson and Jeannie that he had gone to England following a job offer.

Almost all of this description of the death of David Wright and the concealment of his body comes of course from Roy Fontaine as no-one else was present but Wright and he wasn't in able to say what happened. Roy certainly told several different versions of the story – for example, in one version he claimed that he had started work at Kirtleton House much earlier in the year and that the murder took place in July. However, in most versions he claims November and notes that the reason that he couldn't just bury the body was that the ground was frozen and that is the version I have used here. When the police much later searched Roy's room in Kirtleton House, they found blood stains on the mattress of Roy's bed, but it was not possible to be certain that these were from Wright or whether they had anything to do with his death.

With Wright's body hidden, it looked as if Roy was safe in Kirtleton House until, just a few days after the murder, Lady Hudson received an anonymous telephone call. Roy, listening in on an extension, heard a voice he recognized tell his employer that her butler was a thief, a con-man and an ex-convict and that she was in extreme danger. The voice was that of Colin, Hazel's son who had somehow discovered where Roy was working.

Lady Hudson called in the police. There had been no thefts from the house and no-one suspected that the absence of

David Wright was ominous, so Roy was simply asked to leave Kirtleton House. He was even able to demand three months salary in lieu of notice. He then headed south, but only as far as a small village, Newton Arlosh, just over the border in Cumbria in England. He took a three month rental on a cottage there while he worked out what to do next. He told his landlords that he was a writer who wanted some peace and quiet to work on his next book.

Photo: Chris Heaton

However, the only writing he did at the cottage was the preparation of job applications. He was surprised and delighted when, after only a week or so, his impeccable references secured him a new job as a butler, this time working for Sir Walter Scott-Elliot in his flat in Sloane Square in London. Sir Walter was eighty-two years old, an ex-soldier and MP but drifting inevitably and slowly towards complete senility and reliant on the daily ingestion of strong pain killers (administered by his faithful butler, of course).

Sir Walter did not check Roy's references. He was very wealthy indeed with bank accounts in a number of countries. This time, Roy was confident –his employer's flat was also filled with valuable paintings and other objects d'art. He planned to steal and sell off the items in the flat and to gradually siphon off the old man's wealth from the bank accounts until he had made enough money to retire to somewhere with warm sun and golden beaches. This, he decided, was to be his last and greatest robbery.

The only impediment to this plan was Dorothy Scott-Elliot, Sir Walter's wife of Indian descent, who was just sixty and not in the least senile. However, Dorothy did suffer from chronic arthritis in the damp atmosphere of England and was forced to spend long periods confined to bed. She was also reliant on regular doses of strong pain killers.

Sloane Square

Photo: Thomon

Roy arrived at the flat in Sloane Square and quickly made himself as indispensible as possible. He regularly took Sir Walter shopping and ensured that the confused old gentleman purchased what he actually needed. On one of these shopping expeditions, Roy was left at Harrods when Sir Walter went on with friends. He strolled round the corner to a pub called The Lancelot. There, behind the bar, he met Mary Coggle, the woman which whom he had been having an affair during his marriage to Ruth Holmes and his engagement to Hazel Patterson. Mary had fallen on hard times. Her drinking problems had continued and she was reduced to supplementing her meager salary as a barmaid by occasional prostitution and by selling on stolen credit cards and chequebooks.

She was delighted to see Roy the dapper butler once more. Roy was delighted to see her too, mainly because he had in mind another money-making scheme with which he needed some assistance. He had spent some time surveying the rooftop of the flat on Sloane Square and the roofs of adjacent buildings. It would be possible, he thought, to burgle these other houses by gaining access through narrow skylights. Roy himself was now a little too old and too portly to undertake such an athletic burglary, but he wondered if Mary might know someone who would be interested in helping out? Fortunately, Mary knew just the person: Michael Kitto, a slim, handsome thief and burglar in his early thirties.

Roy met with Kitto and took him back to apartment on Sloane Square (the Scott-Elliots were away for the weekend). Kitto agreed that access from the roof of the flat to nearby houses was indeed possible. Kitto was married with two children but he was also bisexual and he readily agreed to become Roy's lover. The two spent the rest of the weekend in bed, happily interspersing sex with planning burglaries and deciding what to do with the proceeds.

In December, Lady Scott-Elliot was admitted to a clinic for four days to receive treatment for her arthritis. Sir Walter stayed at home, in a pain killer and senility induced haze. On 8th December Roy went out to the pub where he happened to meet Kitto. The young man suggested that perhaps they could return to the flat on Sloane Square together to discuss further details of the planned burglaries? In bed? Roy readily agreed and the two went back together.

Chapter 8: Murder most foul

> *'Lacking the moral centre of gravity that, in people of other personality types, tames the striving for power and directs it toward socially valuable ends.'*

The two men arrived at the flat and went to Roy's room where they continued to drink. When they finished Roy's supply of alcohol, they went to the main cocktail cabinet to get more. On the way, they passed Lady Scott-Elliot's room. To Roy's horror, as they passed, the door opened and there stood Dorothy Scott-Elliot, angrily demanding to know who Kitto was and what he was doing in her flat? The clinic, it seemed, had been so pleased with the progress of her treatment that they had decided to release her a day early.

There was a moment of frozen silence, then Roy knocked the elderly woman to the ground. She was stunned, but not unconscious and she started to struggle to get back to her feet and to shout. Roy picked up a cushion off a sofa and pressed her back down, holding it over her face. She continued to writhe and struggle. Roy knelt on top of her and Kitto helped him press the cushion firmly over her nose and mouth. Finally, her struggles lessened. Roy removed the cushion. She was still panting for breath. She was, as Roy later said, a tough old bird. But that didn't save her. This time, Roy pressed the cushion down as hard as he could whilst Kitto strangled her with his hands. Finally, she stopped struggling. Roy held the cushion in place for some time before cautiously removing it. This time, blood was running freely from her nose, she had stopped breathing and there was no detectable pulse.

The two men looked at the body on the floor. Kitto was horrified. Roy was very angry indeed. He explained that he had devised an elaborate plan to gain power of attorney over the couple's wealth by forging Dorothy's signature. However, he hadn't been able to find a sample of her signature which he could copy, so that plan was now worthless.

Kitto and Roy took the body and put it in her bed. Then Roy went to reassure Sir Walter, who had been woken by the sounds of his wife struggling for her life. Roy assured him that Lady Scott-Elliot had had a bad dream, but that she was now peacefully sleeping. Sir Walter went back to sleep.

Roy and Kitto conferred in Roy's room. It was obvious that the old man would also have to be killed, but Roy was keen to keep him alive as long as possible in the hope that he could devise some method of accessing his employer's bank accounts. The following morning Sir Walter was sent to spend the day at his club, giving Roy a chance to organize for his return.

He contacted Mary Coggle, and she agreed to come to the house to impersonate Lady Scott-Elliot. Sir Walter was plied with whiskey and pain killers as soon as he returned to ensure that he was even more fuddled than usual and, for a couple of days, he seemed to accept that Mary Coggle really was his wife – Roy kept contact between the two to a minimum by telling Sir Walter that his wife was unwell and wanted to stay in bed. The only occasions when Sir Walter saw Coggle, she was wearing a wig and in bed in a semi-darkened bedroom.

On the 12th December, Coggle donned one of Dorothy's wigs and some of her clothes while Sir Walter was at his club. Roy then summoned a representative of a car hire firm to the flat, explaining that the Scott-Elliots wished to hire a car for a trip to Scotland and that he was their godson. Kitto posed as the chauffeur and Coggle impersonated Dorothy, though the person from the hire company was startled to note that she was wearing a fur coat in the well-heated apartment. Coggle was so enamored with the fur coat that she refused to remove it even though she was sweating profusely.

When Sir Walter returned he was once again supplied with whisky and pain killers and told that he was going on a trip to meet members of his family in Scotland. When he was bundled into the car, the effects of the alcohol and drugs were so dramatic that he didn't even recognize that the woman sitting next to him on the back seat of the car was not his wife. He did ask uncertainly whether she had dyed her hair, not realizing that the body of his real wife was wrapped in a blanket in the boot.

Fortunately, the Ford Granada which Roy hired had a large boot.

Photo: Kieran White

They drove to Scotland with Sir Walter dosing happily in the back seat. Roy woke him only once, to get him to sign several blank cheques. They stopped in the border town of Lanark so that Roy could buy a shovel from an ironmongers shop, then they continued towards the Highlands.

In Perthshire, close to village of Braco, they turned off the main road and found a quiet spot to bury Lady Scott-Elliot's body. Kitto and Roy lifted the body out of the boot and tossed it over a low wall. The ground was frozen hard, and all they were able to do was scrape a shallow depression in the ground. They settled for covering the body with branches and undergrowth and drove on north until they reached the town of Blair Atholl.

They checked in to a hotel and, while Roy and Kitto took Sir Walter to his room and put him to bed, Mary Coggle, still pretending to be Lady Scott-Elliot and still wearing her fur coat, proceeded to get happily and completely drunk in the hotel bar. Roy was coming to the conclusion that Mary was rapidly becoming more of a liability than an asset.

The next day, they continued to drive north, passing Inverness and entering bleak countryside and very quiet roads. Roy would periodically waken Sir Walter to make him sign more checks. Then as they were driving on a remote road near Glen Affric in the Highlands during the afternoon of 14th December, the old man petulantly said that he was tired of signing cheques and refused to sign any more. Roy told Kitto to stop the car. The two men half led, half dragged Sir Walter down a steep slope covered with rhododendrons. At the bottom, Roy pushed the frail, confused old man to the ground and strangled him with his woolen scarf. Kitto held Sir Walter's arms until he stopped struggling. Roy kicked the body several times to make sure that he was dead and then the two men began to climb back towards the car.

As they were almost at the car, and to Roy's intense irritation, they heard a groan from below. Roy went to the boot of the car and retrieved the shovel. Then he went back to where the old man lay, ordering Kitto to follow. Sir Walter was still alive and struggling feebly to get to his feet. Roy pushed him down again and then stamped hard on his throat. The old man writhed as Roy put his full weight on his neck. He then passed the shovel to Kitto and told him to use it to smash in Sir Walter's head. Kitto complied. A few moments later, Sir Walter Scott-Elliot lay still, his skull crushed by blows from the shovel. There was no doubt that he was dead this time.

Photo: Richard Webb

They went back to the car where Mary Coggle was finally and thankfully able to remove the wig she had been wearing since they had left London. However, she refused to hand over the fur coat. Roy patiently explained that she couldn't keep the coat as it linked them to the dead couple. Instead, he said that he would sell it and they could split the proceeds. Mary refused to give it to him. She wanted to show it to her friends in London, she explained.

Roy stopped trying to persuade her to give up the coat. Instead, he suggested that the trio should return to London and begin to sell off the items from the Scott-Elliot's flat. They returned to and discovered to their relief that there was no sign of any police activity or anyone looking for the missing couple. They spent the next two weeks selling off as many items of jewellery, paintings and other valuable objects from the flat as they could. They travelled all over England, selling off items to widely separated antiques dealers in order to avoid suspicion.

Chapter 9: A matter of life and death

'Irritability and aggressiveness, as indicated by repeated physical fights or assaults.'

During their travels to sell off the stolen items, they found themselves in the north of England and Roy suggested that they drive to his rented cottage in Newton Arlosh. He still had the keys, the rent had been paid in advance and there was more than a month of the lease left. The remote cottage seemed like a good place to hide-out in safety so the others agreed and Kitto drove them to Cumbria.

For several days Roy had been pondering the problem of what to do about Mary Coggle. Her continuing refusal to give up the fur coat stolen from Dorothy Scott-Elliot was a problem. While they were all together, Roy had been able to keep her under control. When she was alone, and especially if she was drinking (which she very often was), she would be a liability. The haul from selling off the items from the flat was also a little disappointing. If it was split three ways, there simply wasn't enough to fund Roy's retirement in the sun as he had hoped. But if it could be split just two ways...

Kitto, Roy and Mary arrived at the cottage in the early hours of the 15th December. Kitto and Roy had a drink. Mary had been drinking during the journey and was more than a little drunk by the time that they arrived at the cottage. She had sex with both of them and then they began to discuss what to do next. The issue of the fur coat was raised again. Roy insisted again that it was too dangerous for Mary to keep it. Mary said that she was not only going to keep it, she was going to show it off to her friends.

Once again, Roy felt that he had no option. It was, he later said, either her or him. After a heated argument, he struck Mary over the head with the poker, stunning her. She fell to the floor and Roy, with Kitto's assistance, tied her hands behind her back and dragged her over to the sofa. As she begged for her life and promised that she would never betray him, Roy tied a plastic bag over her head. He and Kitto poured themselves drinks and watched as she struggled and suffocated. Finally, she was still and her body was stuffed under one of the beds until morning.

The next day Roy and Kitto bundled the body into the boot of the car. They drove south, stopping to toss Mary's body into a river near the town of Lockerbie. Then they returned to Edinburgh where they abandoned the hire car in a side-street and hired another Ford Granada from a local firm using a stolen driving licence.

When Roy considered how much money the sale of items from the Scott-Elliot's flat had brought in, he knew that he needed at least one more big haul to fund his retirement. He knew just what to do – he and Kitto would return to

Kirtleton House and they would rob Lady Hudson. That would provide sufficient funds and they could then go their separate ways. The only minor issue was that it would be easier with a third person – there might be several members of staff in Lady Hudson's house and controlling them would be easier with a third person. Pondering this they drove south to Staffordshire where Roy had been invited to spend Christmas with his sister Violet and her family.

Roy enjoyed Christmas with Violet and she was impressed with Kitto who she considered of rather better class than Roy's usual criminal friends. However, there was one major irritant for Roy – Violet had also invited Donald to her home for Christmas. Roy still loathed Donald and still suspected him of twice informing on him, though he had no proof of this.

When he arrived, Donald explained that he had recently been released from prison, this time for an attempted sexual assault on a young girl. He was looking for work, though he hadn't been able to find anything so far. This gave Roy an idea. Donald wasn't especially bright, but he wasn't troubled about breaking the law and he would do what he was told. Out of earshot of Violet and her husband, Roy explained to Donald that he and Kitto were planning a robbery together and asked if he wanted to take part?

Donald was delighted – his own criminal career to date had been entirely petty and he hoped that by joining up with his older brother he might be able to move up into another league. He happily accepted the offer.

While Roy, Donald and Violet were enjoying their family get-together in Staffordshire, a young farm worker called Duncan Kerr was having a rather less pleasant Christmas Day. He was driving his tractor on a small bridge over the Black Burn near Lockerbie when he noticed something in the water below. He got out to look and realised that he was looking at the bloodied body of a woman, wedged between two rocks. He called the police and the body was removed from the burn and taken to the mortuary. Though no-one yet realised it, the body of Mary Coggle had been found.

Photo: Mike Pennington

At the same time, police were called by an antiques dealer in Newcastle-Under-Lyme who had been approached by two men who had tried to sell him valuable items at suspiciously low prices. The man guessed that the items were stolen and informed the police. He had also noted the number plate of the car the men were driving and this was traced to a car-hire company in London. The car had been found abandoned in a street in Edinburgh and the address for the hire was that of the Scott-Elliot's flat in Sloane Square.

Police went to the flat and discovered that it had been completely ransacked and all items of value removed. Questioning of neighbours and friends revealed that no-one had seen the elderly couple since mid-December. A forensic examination found traces of Dorothy's blood in her bedroom which raised the suspicion of foul play. Police also noted that no-one had seen the Scott-Elliots' well-spoken new butler since the couple had vanished and they were very interested in talking to him.

Unaware of these developments and after staying with Violet for a few days, Roy, Donald and Kitto set off to drive up to the Scottish Borders for their raid on Kirtleton House. They reached Carlisle on New Year's Day and checked in to a hotel. It was then that Roy noticed for the first time that their new hire car had the numbers 999 in its registration number. In an uncharacteristic fit of superstition he raged that this wouldn't do – 999 was the number used to summon the police in an emergency and it was surely unlucky to have that number on their car. Roy insisted that Kitto steal a set of numberplates that evening and put them on the car, an act that would lead to his eventual capture.

Kitto fitted the stolen numberplates to the car the next morning and they set off towards Roy's rented cottage in Newton Arlosh in Cumbria. The weather was bad with heavy snow and the cottage would provide a safe and discreet place to wait before they risked the drive to Kirtleton House. During their short stay at the cottage, Roy became increasingly irritated with his brother and he began to regret taking him along.

On the 14th January, the three men retired to the local pub, the Joiner's Arms, to enjoy a few drinks. Donald had more than a few and soon he was boasting to other people in the bar that he and his brother were on their way north to pull off "*a big job*". Disgusted by his brother's inability to keep his mouth shut, Roy suggested that it was time to return to the cottage where they could continue to drink for free.

Roy made sure that Donald had plenty to drink when they arrived back at the cottage and listened carefully as his brother explained that, during his last visit to prison, he had been shown an effective way to tie someone up which required very little rope. Given that it was likely that Lady Hudson and her staff would need to be restrained during the robbery, Roy agreed that this sounded interesting and asked whether Donald would be willing to demonstrate the technique? Rope was produced and Donald volunteered to be tied-up while he explained the new procedure to Roy. When he was bound hand and foot and completely helpless, Roy asked whether Kitto had heard what Donald had said in the pub? Kitto agreed that he had. His brother, Roy said meaningfully, was just like Mary. Kitto agreed.

Donald, finally beginning to feel nervous despite his ingestion of alcohol, asked to be untied. Instead, Roy went to his luggage and produced a small bottle of chloroform and a pad which he had brought along to be used on the planned robbery victims. Kitto held Donald down while Roy pressed the chloroform soaked pad over his brother's face.

If a chloroformed pad is held over someone's face for a short time it will render them unconscious. If it is kept there for too long, it can kill. Roy continued to press the pad on to his brother's face long after he had stopped struggling. When he finally removed it, Donald was dead. The two men put him into the bath (Roy said that this would prevent the onset of rigor mortis and make it easier to handle the body the following day). Then, they went to bed.

The next morning, Donald's body was stuffed into the boot

of the car and Roy and Kitto set off north for Kirtleton House, intending to dump the body en-route.

Chapter 10: Beyond a reasonable doubt

'Impulsivity or failure to plan ahead.'

Kitto drove east from the cottage, on narrow, twisting roads and it was late afternoon before they found themselves heading north on the A1 towards the Scottish border. It had also started snowing and, as they approached North Berwick, they agreed that it would probably be safer to spend the night in a hotel and carry on the next day rather than to risk getting stuck. Carrying a dead body in the boot had become so routine for both men now that neither though it necessary to dispose of Donald first – that could always be done in the morning. They parked outside the Blenheim House Hotel in North Berwick and wandered inside.

They checked in as brothers, Roy and Robin Thompson, and explained to the manager, Norman Wright, that they were actually heading for Australia and were planning to catch a flight from Edinburgh. Mr Wright noted that they had only a single, small bag between two of them, which struck him as odd for two people planning to travel to another continent. When Kitto signed the register the manager also noticed that he hesitated first, almost as if he was trying to remember what his name was. The two men dropped off their bags in their room and then went to the dining room and ordered brandies.

Photo: John Chroston

The manager, now very suspicious, went outside to the car-park and looked at their car. He quickly noticed that the registration number on their number plate did not match the registration number on their tax disk. Now certain that there was something suspicious about his new guests, Mr Wright called the police.

When the police arrived, Kitto and Roy were eating their evening meal. The police looked at the car and then entered the hotel to talk to the two guests. They explained about the discrepancy in registration numbers between the number plate and the tax disk. Roy calmly told them that the car was hired and that there must be some mistake. He even asked the two policemen if they would each care for a brandy? They refused, but they were so impressed by Roy's confident demeanor that they waited while he and Kitto finished their meals before taking them to the police station for questioning. It would be the last meal that Roy Fontaine would ever eat as a free man.

Before they could be taken to North Berwick Police station, Roy asked if he could use the toilet in the hotel. Still suspecting nothing, to two police officers agreed. Roy managed to wriggle out of a small window in the toilet and hail a passing taxi. Within a short time, the taxi was speeding him towards Edinburgh. Meanwhile the police had discovered not only that Roy had escaped, they had also found Donald's body, still trussed and wrapped in a plastic sheet in the boot of the car. An all-points bulletin was sent out to stop Roy escaping and road blocks were set up on all major roads.

Roy's taxi got as far as Haddington on the outskirts of Edinburgh before it was stopped at a police road block. As soon as the police saw him, he was recognized, taken back into custody and returned to North Berwick (though he insisted on paying the taxi driver). He was told about the discovery of the body in the boot of the car. He denied knowing anything about it. Then he was told that Kitto had made a full confession which not only implicated him in this murder, it also told about three others. Roy Fontaine finally realized that there was no way out. He thought for a short time before saying that it wasn't four murders actually, it was five. He then proceeded to provide them with a full confession not only to the murders but to a number of thefts and deceptions of which they were not aware.

Detective Chief Inspector Shearer, the officer leading the investigation, spent a great deal of time interviewing Roy and concluded that he was the oddest character the policeman had ever encountered. Roy displayed no emotion at all as he described the murders and showed nothing as he later took the police to the locations where the bodies of David Wright and Dorothy and Walter Scott-Elliot had been concealed. The only feeling that Roy appeared to have was satisfaction that his crimes were being widely reported in the press. This was, he told police, the biggest case they would ever be involved in. Despite his seeming lack of emotion, Roy twice attempted to commit suicide while awaiting trial. In both cases he took an overdose of sleeping tablets he had somehow been able to acquire from other prisoners.

In the summer of 1978, Roy Fontaine and Michael Kitto

each received two life sentences at the Crown Court in Edinburgh for the murders of David Wright and Sir Walter Scott-Elliot. In September they were then taken to the Old Bailey in London to face trial for the murder of Lady Dorothy Scott-Elliot. At the second trial, Roy was furious to discover the Kitto was to be defended by John Mortimer, QC, the creator of the fictional Rumpole of the Bailey and already a celebrity. If there was to be a celebrity barrister involved in the trial, Roy felt that it should be his. Roy was even more incensed when he was referred to as Archibald Hall throughout both trials though, fortunately, no-one called him Archie.

The Old Bailey

Photo: Tbmurray

John Mortimer introduced an interesting argument in his defence of Kitto – he claimed that his client was a *'passive homosexual'* who was so dominated and controlled by Roy that he was unable to distinguish right from wrong. Roy generally relied throughout the trial on claiming either that he had acted in self defence (in the case of David Wright) or that the murders he committed with Kitto were either done at Kitto's instigation or that Kitto committed these murders by himself.

The jury were unimpressed by either approach and both Roy and Kitto were found guilty and sentenced to life imprisonment. The judge recommended that Kitto serve at least fifteen years. He recommended that Roy should never be released from prison. The Home Office concurred. In 1983 a new mechanism was introduced in UK Law where a person could be convicted to remain in prison until they died. This new tariff (which became known as the Whole Life Tariff) was applied to a very small number of notorious murderers in British prisons. A prisoner serving a whole life tariff cannot be released without the explicit intervention of the Home Secretary. To date, this has not happened.

Prisoners detained under a whole life tariff have included the Moors murderers Ian Brady and Myra Hindley, serial killers Peter Sutcliffe and Dennis Nilsen, murderous Doctor Harold Shipman and Roy Fontaine.

Chapter 11: Fade Out

> *'Being indifferent to the feelings and needs of others.'*

Roy was initially sent to Wandsworth prison in London before being transferred to Wing C at Full Sutton near York where he shared the *'lifer's wing'* with other murderers including Dennis Nilsen. Once settled into the routine of prison, Roy quickly became known as *'Roy the Boy'* to both staff and fellow prisoners. Almost incredibly, a regular visitor in the early days of his imprisonment was Ruth Holmes, the woman he had married in 1972 and divorced in 1973.

Whatever else prison may have done for Roy Fontaine, it didn't appear to diminish his hunger for notoriety or his wish to play the leading role in the movie that was his life. He remained an inveterate publicity hound and gave a number of interviews to newspapers. In 1981 the first book about him, *The Butler: The Life of Archibald Thompson Hall* by James Copeland, was published. Roy provided assistance to the author and was listed as the co-author of this work which provided a brief and not very satisfactory précis of his life and crimes.

In November 1992, Michael Kitto was released from prison after having served fifteen years.

Roy clearly didn't feel that the first book about him was good enough because in early 1993, he called Paul Pender, a young scriptwriter working for BBC Scotland. Pender had written the screenplay for *The Bogie Man*, a popular television play broadcast over Christmas 1992 and starring Robbie Coltraine as a man who escapes from a mental hospital believing that he is Humphrey Bogart. Roy liked the play and decided that Pender would be just the person to write a screenplay or book based on his life. Pender visited Roy a number of times in Full Sutton during 1993 and produced copious notes for what would become *The Butler Did It: My True and Terrifying Encounters with a Serial Killer*. However, to Roy's intense irritation, Pender went on to a career as a successful Hollywood screenwriter and the book wasn't completed and published until 2012.

In 1995, the *Observer* newspaper published a letter from Roy in which he requested the right to die. He did this on several occasions though most people who knew him suggested that this was done as much for the publicity it would surely bring as it was a reflection on his part of a decision to kill himself. He was by this point almost seventy years old and by some margin the oldest prisoner serving a whole life tariff.

In 1996 a book titled *On Trial for Murder* by Wynn Douglas was published. This compendium of reports on famous UK murder trials included a factual and rather dry section on the trial of Roy and Kitto.

In 1999 Roy, presumably unhappy because the book by Paul Pender had not yet appeared, published his autobiography, *A Perfect Gentleman*. This was written with the assistance of professional crime writer Trevor Anthony Holt and has become used as a primary source by many people writing about Roy, but this book is an idealized (from Roy's point of view, at least) version of his story. In every case, he is caught in his confidence tricks or scams because of the failure of someone else or because of sheer, blind, bad luck, never because of his own inept and blundering behavior. Every scene features Roy as the principal and most fascinating character. In terms of the five murders, it is carefully explained how each was forced upon him:

- David Wright prompted his own murder by stealing from Lady Hudson and then attempting to shoot Roy.
- Lady Dorothy Scott-Elliot forced Roy and Kitto to murder her when she unexpectedly saw them together in her apartment in Sloane Square.
- Sir Walter Scott-Elliot had to be killed because of the murder of his wife.
- Mary Coggle precipitated her own murder by

refusing to give up the fur coat to which she had become so attached.

- Donald Hall had to be killed after boasting in the local pub of the big job that he and his brother were about to pull off.

In every case, Roy describes how he was forced against his will to commit these murders. Which of course means that really, he isn't to blame at all. It's the classic defense of the psychopath – they don't want to do bad things, but circumstances conspire to force them. And even then, it's clear that they don't feel that the things they have done are really reprehensible. Much later, Roy attempted to classify the murders (other than the murder of Wright which he said was self-defense) as *'mercy killings'* – he explained that Walter Scott-Elliot was suffering from advanced dementia, Dorothy was in acute pain from arthritis and he saved Mary Coggle from a life of prostitution.

After his autobiography was published, Roy also claimed to have killed more than five people – he said in an interview that he had also murdered an American helicopter pilot and a man who worked in a petrol station. However, he was unable to provide any details of these killings and most people believed that these claims were untrue and just another example of Roy attempting to make himself seem more dramatic and more interesting.

Roy clearly continued to believe that he was not just fascinating but that he was also a basically good person who had, unfortunately, made a couple of mistakes. In 1999 he was transferred to Kingston Prison in Portsmouth where he spent much of his time campaigning to have his whole life tariff removed. He appealed to courts in the UK and to the European Court of Human Rights, claiming that the tariff was inhumane.

HM Prison Kingston

Photo: Basher Eyre

On 16th September 2002, while waiting for the latest debate in Europe on the Whole Life Tariff, Roy Fontaine died of a stroke in his cell at Kingston prison in Portsmouth at the age of seventy-eight. At the time of his death, Roy was one of the oldest prisoners in any British prison and the oldest Whole Life Tariff prisoner.

One month after his death the European Court of Human Rights completed its review of the UK whole Life Tariff and concluded that it was neither inhumane or unjust.

In 2002 the publicity surrounding the death of Roy Fontaine brought his case to the attention of actor Malcolm McDowell, the star who became famous for his leading role in the controversial 1970s film Clockwork Orange. McDowell wanted to make Monster Butler, a film based on Roy's life with himself playing the lead role. By July 2012, a cast had been assembled (including Gary Oldman in a role based on the character of John Wooton), sets had been built and filming was ready to begin at Gosford House in East Lothian. Had he still been alive, Roy would doubtless have been breathless with excitement. Then filming was delayed for one week due to financial problems. Then for another week. Then another and at each stage, technicians were asked to continue working and were assured that they would be paid as soon as filming actually began.

Unfortunately, that never happened and the production finally ground to a halt in acrimony and ill-feeling, leaving hundreds of thousands of pounds in unpaid salaries and expenses. It appears that confident assertions that the money would be available were nothing more than wishful thinking and there are those who believe that the whole episode was no more than a confidence trick. Fingers were pointed at everyone from McDowell himself to Dark House Films, a Canadian production company which was behind financing for the project. There does not seem to have ever been any final resolution to who was to blame for what and arguments and accusations about unpaid bills continue to reverberate.

Malcolm McDowell

Photo: GabboT

There have been sightings of the ghostly figure of a man who seems to be wearing a butler's uniform at a ruined house in Glen Affric, not far from where Roy and Michael

Kitto murdered Sir Walter Scott-Elliot. There are those who believe that this is the ghost of Roy Fontaine, though it has never been explained why his spirit would choose this particular spot to manifest.

Conclusion

Roy Fontaine stopped killing only because he was caught due to his own erratic behavior and complacency. If he had not been arrested, there seems little doubt that he would have killed again. There is certainly little question that he planned to kill Michael Kitto as soon as his help was no longer needed. Kitto himself later said that he realized this and planned to run off with his share of the loot from the robbery of Kirtleton House as soon as he could.

It also seems likely that, if the robbery at Kirtleton House had gone ahead, Roy would have been unwilling to leave any potential witnesses in the house alive. He had by that time killed five people in a little over two months and it seems unlikely that he would have baulked at more killing. His confederate Kitto also seems to have been entirely willing to go along with any murder proposed by his partner and had already assisted with four of the killings.

But just what was it that prompted Roy Fontaine to begin killing in November 1977 after a long but notably violence-free criminal career? That initially appears to be the most significant question about this case, but perhaps looking at it in this way is actually misleading. Perhaps a better question might be: what took Roy Fontaine so long to start killing?

The con-tricks, robberies and deceptions that Roy practiced for most of his life were based upon complete indifference to the suffering or fate of his victims. Things like his impersonation of Sheik Medinah may seem bold, ingenious and perhaps even amusing. But the truth is that all the crimes that he committed were based on the presupposition that whatever Roy wanted, he had a right to take from those weaker, more credulous or more trusting than himself. Roy Fontaine felt no remorse for those he robbed and no pangs of conscience for those he deceived.

By any rational analysis, Roy Fontaine's actions show that he fitted most definitions of the psychopath long before he killed anyone. Therefore, in November 1977, when he first robbed a man of his life, it should not be a surprise that he felt no pang of remorse for this act either.

After that, when he discovered not only that he was capable of killing but was also able to get away with it, this must have seemed like the answer to his prayers. He was able to rob the apartment of the Scott-Elliots in London more completely and more efficiently than ever before. Why? Because they were dead and unable to interfere. In late 1977 the scales dropped from Roy Fontaine's eyes. He no longer needed to trust to luck or to hope that his deception wouldn't be discovered too soon. Killing was easy and it solved all his problems. All he had to do was continue to kill to ensure that he would be both wealthy and secure.

When Mary Coggle proved to be a potential threat, he killed her without compunction and then spent the night sleeping peacefully in the bed under which her body was hidden. When he was unsure if he could trust his brother, he adopted what was rapidly becoming his default solution to any uncertainty – he killed him.

There can be no doubt that he would have continued to kill if he had been given the opportunity. His ability to impersonate and to improvise a convincing story on the spot when required would have made him very difficult to catch. The only thing that stopped him was his own over-confidence. For most people, if moral scruples don't prevent them from murder, the fear of being caught usually does. Few of us would be able to rest easy in a hotel if we knew that the murdered body of a close relative was hidden in the boot of a car parked outside. For Roy Fontaine, the carrying of bodies in boots had become so routine by January 1978 that he no longer even worried about it.

It was this combination of a lack of moral inhibitions and a lack of fear that he would be caught that allowed Roy to commit murder. However, this fatal hubris was also what led directly to his arrest and final imprisonment.

There are those who argue that a whole life tariff, confining a person to prison for the remainder of their life, is an inhuman act. In the case of Roy Fontaine, this was nothing more than an act of sensible self-defence on the part of the rest of society. If freed, there is very little doubt that Roy Fontaine would have killed again if he felt this was necessary and that he could have got away with it. Beneath the veneer of an obsequious butler, this man was a ruthless, brutal and emotionless killer who had finally discovered his life's vocation and reveled in the notoriety it brought him. He was so completely unable to feel pity or remorse that he simply couldn't understand why other people might not be charmed and entranced by him.

When Roy Fontaine met with BBC script writer Paul Pender in 1999, he hoped that Pender would write either a screenplay or a book about his life. However, he didn't want to make this just another true crime story. At their last meeting, he begged Pender to *"show the funny side of me as well."* Because that was still how Roy Fontaine saw himself, as a charming rogue filled with funny stories and mordant wit. When Paul Pender asked how he could do this given that Roy was also a multiple murderer, he seemed puzzled.

Because to Roy Fontaine, those murders weren't really all that important - they were no more significant than the deaths of secondary characters in a movie. Roy, the star performer in the drama that was his own life, didn't want anything to distract the audience from his own performance. He certainly didn't want anyone to invest emotionally in the people he killed, people he saw as unimportant, because that might distract attention from him.

Roy Fontaine was the complete embodiment of the psychopath (or an example of an anti-social personality or a sociopath depending on which psychological terminology you prefer). For all his posturing as a man of culture, refinement and taste, he was one of the most brutal murderers in Scottish criminal history.

I hope you enjoyed reading this book. If you did, please take a moment to leave me a review on Amazon. Your opinion matters and positive reviews help me greatly. Thank you.

I also welcome feedback from readers. If you have comments on this book or ideas for other books in the Murder World series, please send me an email at: stevemac357@gmail.com.

Bibliography

Autobiography

Roy Fontaine's autobiography has had as many different names as the man himself. When it was first published, this book was given the relatively low-key title *'A Perfect Gentleman'* and the author's name was given as *Roy Archibald Hall*. It's odd to see the use of the hated *'Archibald'* as the author's name – presumably Roy or his publisher was worried that if the author's name was given as *'Roy Hall'* or *'Roy Fontaine'*, people wouldn't associate this book with the sensational trial and conviction of Archibald Thompson Hall? When a new edition appeared soon after Roy's death in 2002, it retained the same author name but was re-titled to the more dramatic: *'To Kill and Kill Again: The Chilling True Confessions of a Serial Killer'*. In 2011 it was re-published yet again, this time with the title: *'The Wicked Mr Hall: The Memoirs of the Butler Who Loved to Kill.'*

Biographies

The very first true crime biography of Roy Fontaine was *'The Butler: The Life of Archibald Thompson Hall'* (also known as *The Prison Cell Confessions of Archibald Thompson Hall*) by James Copeland which was published in 1981, just three years after his conviction. This book lists

A.T. Hall as co-author and it was produced with the assistance of prison interviews with Roy. It provides a brief overview of the life and crimes of Roy, though it is obvious that he is the source of most of the material

'The Monster Butler: Inside the Mind of a Serial Killer' by Allan Nicol was published in 2011 and is an attempt to look beyond Roy Fontaine's self-serving pronouncements to establish what actually happened. This is probably the most detailed and objective book on this case to date and it rightly points out that there are several conflicting versions of almost every story told by Fontaine.

'The Butler Did It: My True and Terrifying Encounters with a Serial Killer' by Paul Pender was based on a series of interviews given by Roy to then BBC scriptwriter Paul Pender during 1993. However, the book wasn't completed and published until 2012. For the most part, Roy repeated to Pender the same stories which would later appear in his autobiography though with just enough difference to suggest that these are based as much on fantasy and later embellishment as on a real recollection of events. The book is fairly well written and Pender is more than astute enough to recognize precisely what Roy was doing.

'Til Murder Do Us Part: 15 Couples Who Killed' by William Webb was published in 2013 and is an account of various couples who committed murders together. One section of

the book looks at the murders committed by Archibald Thompson Hall and Michael Kitto.

About the Author

Steve MacGregor is a Scot who writes non-fiction on a range of topics including true crime and the paranormal. He has been interested in crime writing since he read his first true crime book at the local library in 1971, when everyone thought he was studying for his homework. Now he doesn't have to do it in secret anymore and reads a range of work by various crime writers.

He is married with two grown-up children and currently lives in Andalucía in Spain.

Other Murder World Scotland books

If you enjoyed this book, you may also be interested in these other Murder World Scotland Books which are also available on Amazon:

Death in a cold town: The Arlene Fraser case

One Morning in April 1998, attractive mother and housewife Arlene Fraser called her children's school in the town of Elgin on the Moray coast of Scotland. She wanted to know what time her son would be returning from a school trip? That was the last time that anyone had contact with Arlene. When a friend arrived at her house two hours later, she found no sign of Arlene and no-one has seen her since.

The search for Arlene Fraser became one of the biggest and longest running missing person cases ever seen in Scotland but no clue was found to indicate what had happened to her. Was she abducted and murdered on the instructions of Nat, her estranged husband as the police claimed? Did she run away to a new life, leaving her children, her home and her friends behind? Was she somehow involved in smuggling?

This book provides a detailed look at Arlene Fraser's disappearance, the trials and the legal maneuvering and appeals which followed. It also analyses the main theories of what may have happened to Arlene to assess which is the most likely.

A killing at kinky cottage: The murder of Max Garvie

The Swinging sixties eventually reached even the tranquil Howe O' the Mearns in the North-East of Scotland. Millionaire farmer Max Garvie and his glamorous wife Sheila became so well-known for their nudist and sex parties that their farmhouse became known locally as '*kinky cottage.*'

However, beneath the swinging exterior, all was not well in the marriage of Max and Sheila. Max was easily bored and constantly sought new sexual adventures and partners. Sheila was interested in a more stable and lasting relationship, but not with Max.

Then, one evening in May 1968, the peace and quiet of this tranquil farming community was ripped apart by a shotgun blast. It seemed that Sheila had finally found a permanent way to solve her marital problems. But was it really that simple?

The Vanishing: The Renee MacRae case

One November evening in 1976, Renee MacRae, the estranged wife of a millionaire Scottish businessman, set off from her luxury home in Inverness. She was going, she had told her husband, to spend the weekend with her sister in Kilmarnock and she took her three year old son Andrew with her.

Four hours later her BMW car was found burning in a remote lay-by on the A9, the main road to the south from Inverness. In the car there was no sign of Renee, Andrew or their luggage.

Police enquiries quickly discovered that Renee's real reason for leaving Inverness was very different to the story she had told her estranged husband and discovered that her life was rather more complicated than it appeared from the outside. The search for the missing mother and son was huge and this became the longest running missing person investigation in Scottish history. Despite this, no trace of Renee or Andrew was ever found.

Officially, Renee MacRae is still missing and no-one has ever been charged with her murder or that of her son. However, over the forty years that have passed since she vanished, tantalizing clues have emerged that allow us to consider the various theories, to work out the most likely course of events that November night and to identify the person most likely to have caused the disappearance.

The face of Bible John: The search for a Scottish serial killer

Just like any other country, Scotland has its share of unsolved crimes. However, few have proved to be as enduringly fascinating as the story of the man who became known as Bible John and who killed at least three women in Glasgow in the late 1960s.

This murderer picked up each of his three known victims at the Barrowland Ballroom in the east of the city centre. The bodies of all three women were later found dumped. All three were mothers, all had been menstruating at the time of their death and all were beaten, raped and strangled. In each case, pieces of the women's clothing vanished.

The murderer made no attempt to conceal or disguise himself and was seen by a number of witnesses at the ballroom and outside - one witness actually shared a taxi with the killer and one of his victims. Through discussions with these witnesses, a well-known artist working on behalf of the police produced a striking portrait of a man with red hair and blue/grey eyes and wearing a cold, rather supercilious expression. This portrait was widely publicized and became known as the face of Bible John. People wondered how the man could possibly avoid arrest with his likeness on the front of every major Scottish newspaper and on police posters throughout the city?

How was this be possible? The murderer frequented a busy public place and was seen with all his victims by a number of witnesses who got a good look at him. By the time of the third murder, there had been massive publicity and people were on their guard and actually looking for a potential killer. Given that, just how did this person manage to kill three times and yet still escape detection? Having killed three times, why did he stop? Did he really stop at all or did he just become more adept at hiding his crimes? Perhaps most importantly of all, did Bible John really exist at all or was he nothing more than an urban myth?

Printed in Great Britain
by Amazon